The Crazy World series (Hardback £3.99) There are now 16 different titles in this best-selling cartoon series – one of them must be right for a friend of yours ...

The Crazy World of Birdwatching (Peter Rigby)
The Crazy World of Gardening (Bill Stott)
The Crazy World of Golf (Mike Scott)
The Crazy World of the Handyman (Roland Fiddy)
The Crazy World of Jogging (David Pye)
The Crazy World of Love (Roland Fiddy)
The Crazy World of Marriage (Bill Stott)
The Crazy World of Music (Bill Stott)
The Crazy World of the Office (Bill Stott)
The Crazy World of Photography (Bill Stott)
The Crazy World of Rugby (Bill Stott)
The Crazy World of Sailing (Peter Rigby)
The Crazy World of Sex (David Pye)
The Crazy World of Skiing (Craig Peterson & Jerry Emerson)
The Crazy World of Tennis (Peter Rigby)

Published in Great Britain in 1988 by Exley Publications Ltd, 16 Chalk Hill, Watford, Herts WD1 4BN, United Kingdom.

ISBN 1-85015-188-1

Printed and bound in Hungary.

the CRAZY world of CATS

Cartoons by
Bill Stott

≣EXLEY

"A whole 25lb turkey? Rubbish! No cat could eat a 25lb turkey..."

"I think that hairdryer is too powerful for him..."

"All that stuff about bringing them gifts – it's rubbish. We do it just to scare them!"

"You must tell me if he's being a nuisance..."

"O.K. a brief explanation will do. Why is my chicken leg in _your_ mouth?"

"An ultimate deterrent eh? Don't make me laugh fellas."

*"Oh come, come – does she look like a cat who'd
make a smell?"*

"'No' is just not in your book is it?"

"How come _I_ get thrown out when the flea was found on the <u>carpet</u>?"

"You're sitting in his chair..."

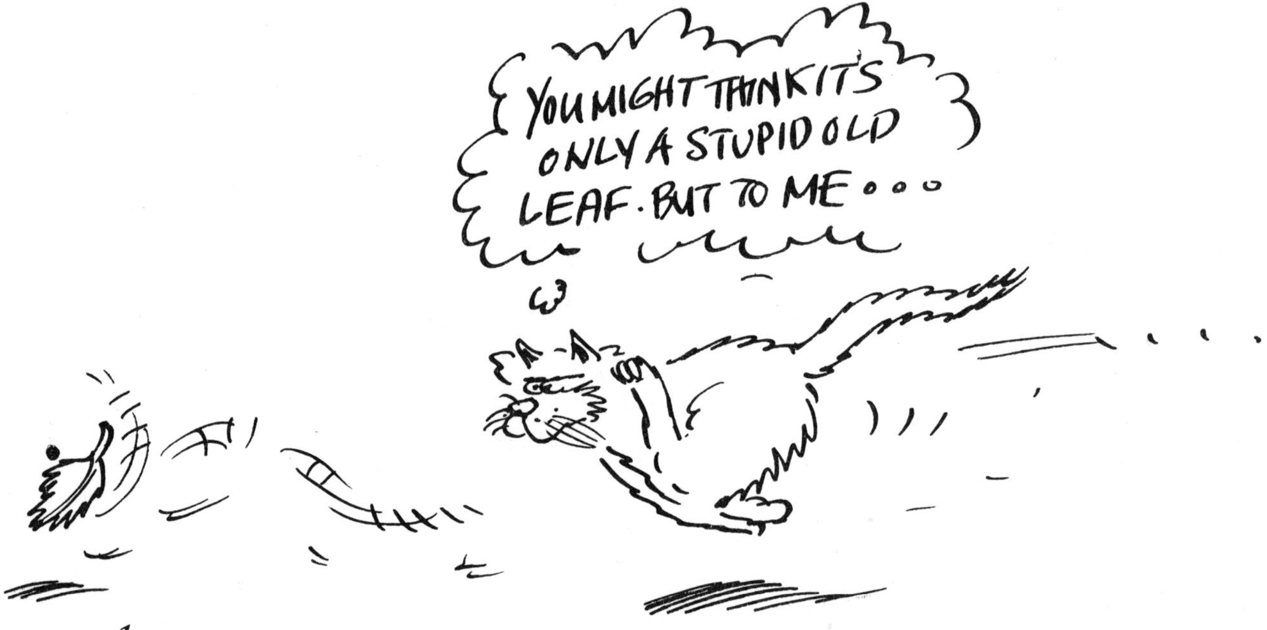
YOU MIGHT THINK IT'S ONLY A STUPID OLD LEAF. BUT TO ME...

2

WHO'S A LOVELY OLD PUSS-CAT?
I AM, BUT GO EASY ON THE SQUEEZING – I HAD AN ESPECIALLY RICH DINNER . . .

"No more aimless yowling for us – I photocopied the words."

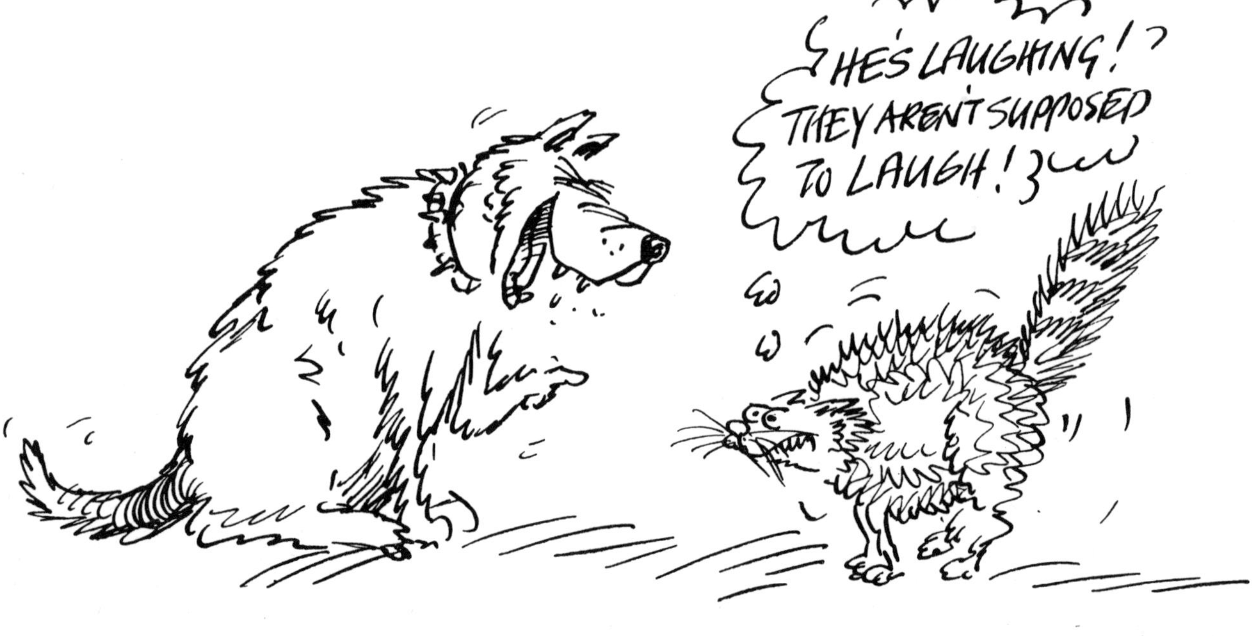
HE'S LAUGHING! THEY AREN'T SUPPOSED TO LAUGH!

"For every ten labels she collects, she gets a free can..."

"Gran! Oscar doesn't seem too keen on 'Kittichews'."

"*Have another go, Son – she's just playing hard to get...*"

"Don't be alarmed. It's just his way of saying
'please don't hurt me.'"

"Play with the yarn. Don't kill it!"

"*What a coward! He's telling me the canary clawed the couch.*"

HELLO! IS MUMA'S DARLING PLEASED TO SEE HER?
OH MY GOD – THEY ATE GREEK AGAIN – THE GARLIC!

"*This way I get all the excitement of the flying boot with none of the effort...*"

"That's what I call a cat flap!"

"I don't care how big it is – no cat digs up my veg. twice!"

"*I see Fluffy's been thrown out of the diner again…*"

"Normally I'd have to admit you're a pretty hum-drum
kind of guy. But with that can-opener in your hand,
you're a giant."

"*Well, of course she's growling. You put ketchup on your steak and she hates ketchup.*"

"The twins tried out your home perm kit on Chester."

"Twinkle? What sort of name is Twinkle??"

"There are some <u>very</u> distant relatives of yours on..."

URRRRR...

1

"*Since she stayed at the Hilton, she's become so fastidious…*"

"And when she actually deigns to come home, we'll do our tiger ambush!"

2

"It's as I suspected – the oaf doesn't speak Felinese!"

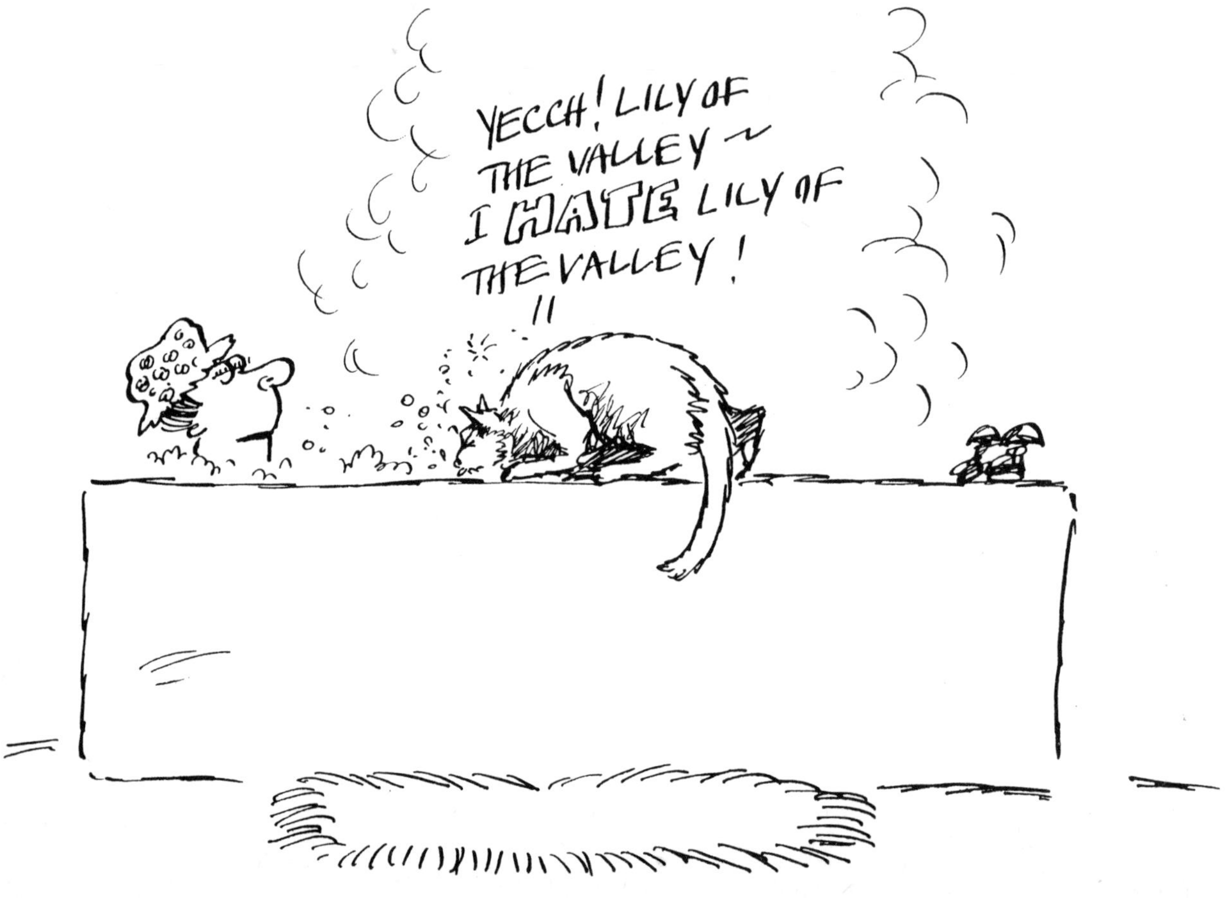
YECCH! LILY OF THE VALLEY ~ I HATE LILY OF THE VALLEY!

UH-UH ~
HE KNOWS IT'S
CHEAP SOYA
SUBSTITUTE!
RIGHT
FIRST TIME!
KITTY

"So much for your independence act!"

"Well, now we've got proof that it's next door's cat that's to blame!"

"*What did the nasty man do to mama's little soldier?*"

"He's got ambitions to play in a jazz band!"

1

2

"Who wants KittiKrunch when you've just eaten six birds?"

"I see that they still haven't fixed the spring on your catflap."

"Hey! There's wild life on this set!"

"You can tell he's a pedigree. He's the only member of the
family who likes politics."

"*I can't teach her that she's not meant to bath in it!*"

"Remember the bird we nearly caught this morning? He's
back – with his big brother..."

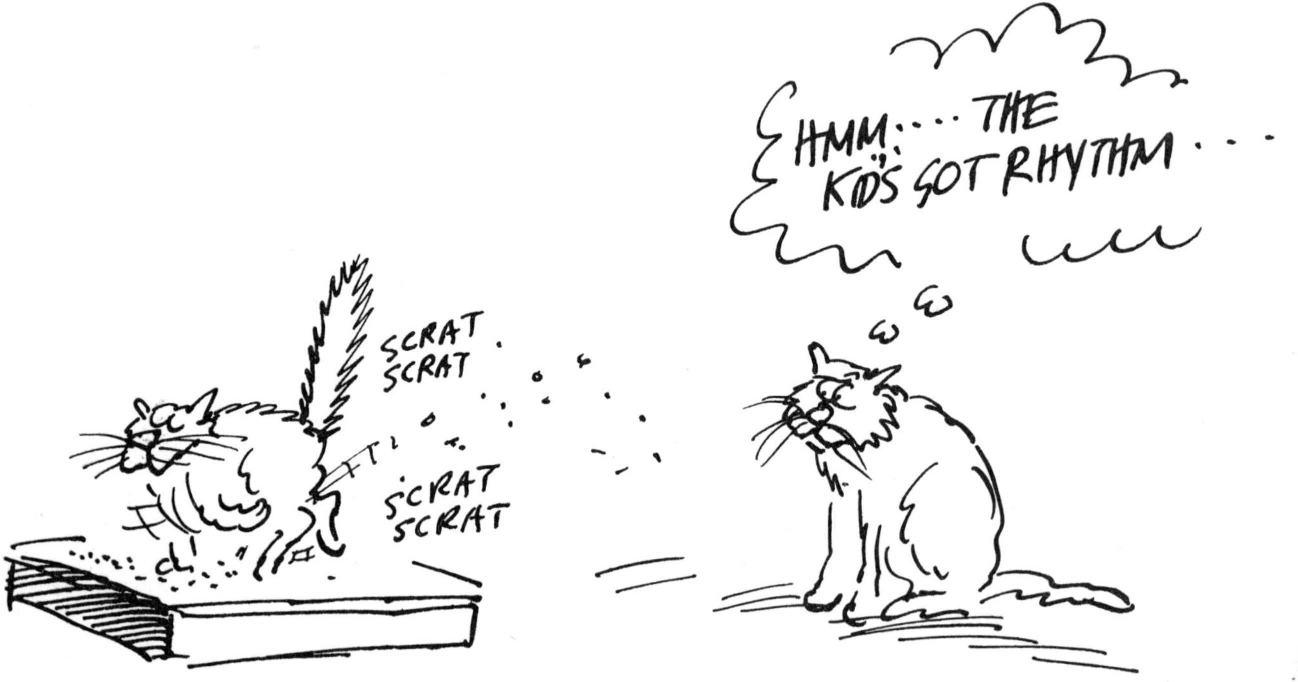
SCRAT
SCRAT
SCRAT
SCRAT
HMM.... THE KID'S GOT RHYTHM...

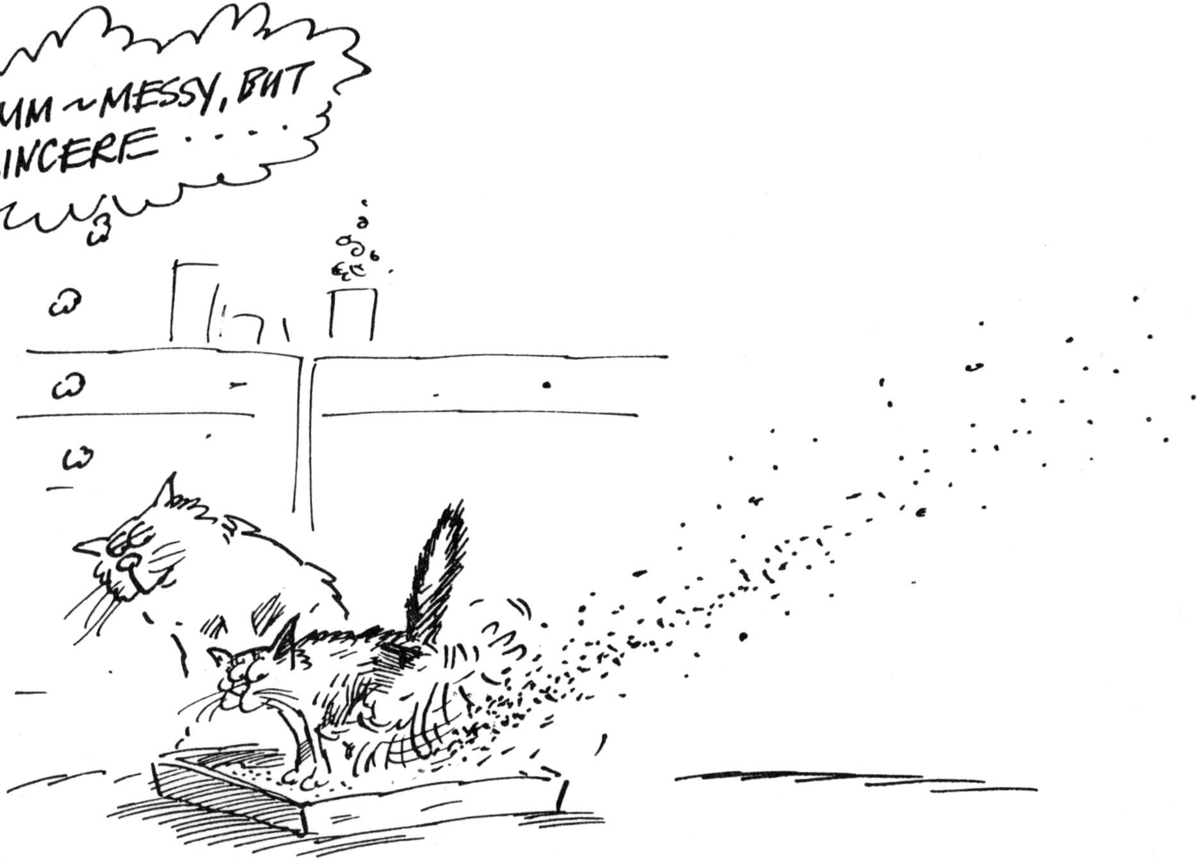
HMM ~ MESSY, BUT SINCERE . . . .

1　　　"He remained motionless, his muscular frame straining,
anticipating the kill..."

2   *"Love those low-flying bumble-bees!"*

"Here Smelly, Smelly. Here Smelly..."

"So he's a little sharp – it beats all that yowling…"

"Do you really think the cat's into practical jokes?"

"Either you come in right now or you're out all night!"

HI ~ MY NAME IS CHESTER, I'M A CAT
AND I'VE COME TO LIVE NEXT DOOR · · ·

1

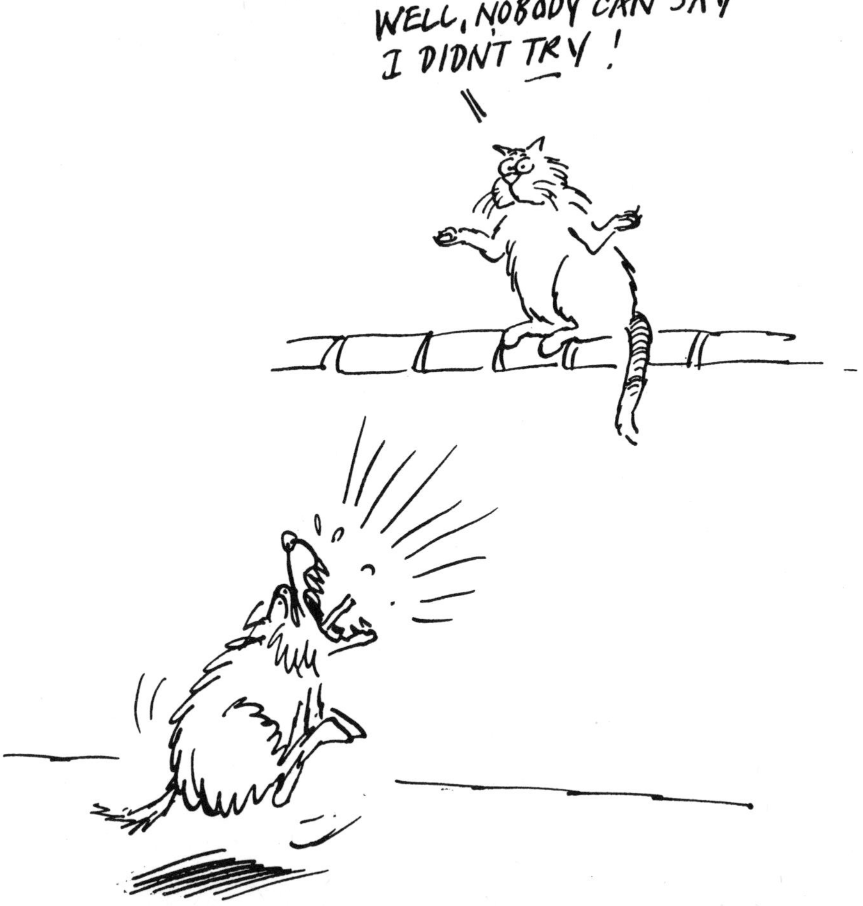
WELL, NOBODY CAN SAY I DIDN'T TRY !

"Harold! Quick! The screens!"

I KNOW, I KNOW —
ITS A SCRATCH POST.
I STILL PREFER THE
WALLPAPER · · · ·

"Don't worry about a thing – I had the operation..."

"Learning to climb trees is cheating!"

"Correct me if I'm wrong, but aren't we black cats supposed to be lucky?"

"What's wrong? He always washes that way – don't they all?"

"Louie, I'd better hang up. They're staring at me the way they always do when I use the 'phone."

"How many times do I have to tell you? Never change channels without asking – it's very rude..."

"... One of our regulars..."

1

"Satisfy my curiosity – if you could get at me, would you actually eat me?"

"A simple 'yes' or 'no' will do."

AH··· AH··· AH······

"*Good, but not <u>that</u> good – checkmate!*"

"How'd you like it if I came and lay on <u>your</u> chest first thing
in the morning?"

"This way, he can enjoy his dreadful country 'n' western without annoying us classical fans…"

"I'll wait until someone comes by before I go and have a drink. I just love those cries of middle class outrage."

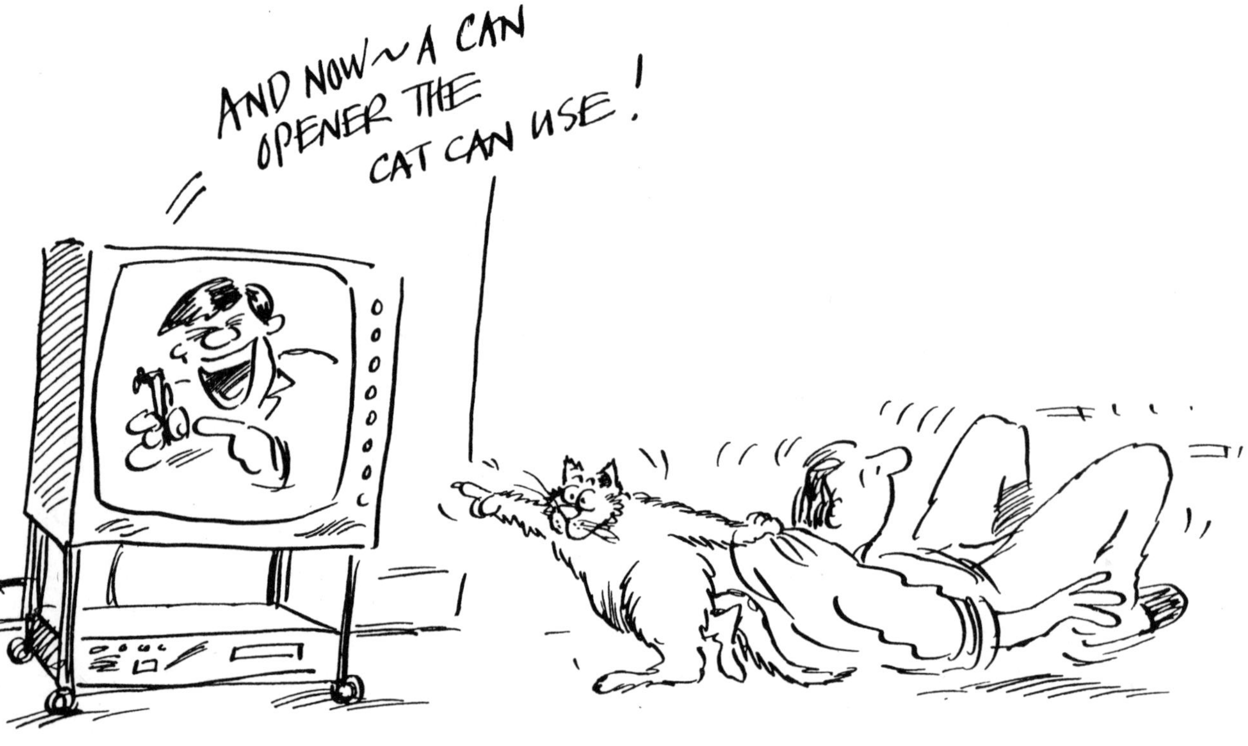
AND NOW ~ A CAN OPENER THE CAT CAN USE !

Other books in the "Crazy World" series:

The Crazy World of Birdwatching. £3.99. By Peter Rigby. Over eighty cartoons on the strange antics of the twitcher brigade. One of our most popular pastimes, this will be a natural gift for any birdwatcher.

The Crazy World of Gardening. £3.99. By Bill Stott. The perfect present for anyone who has ever wrestled with a lawnmower that won't start, over-watered a pot plant or been assaulted by a rose bush from behind.

The Crazy World of Golf. £3.99. By Mike Scott. Over eighty hilarious cartoons show the fanatic golfer in his (or her) every absurdity. What really goes on out on the course, and the golfer's life when not playing are chronicled in loving detail.

The Crazy World of The Handyman. £3.99. By Roland Fiddy. This book is a must for anyone who has ever hung *one* length of wallpaper upside down or drilled through an electric cable. A gift for anyone who has ever tried to "do it yourself" and failed!

The Crazy World of Jogging. £3.99. By David Pye. An ideal present for all those who find themselves running early in the morning in the rain and wondering why they're there. They'll find their reasons, their foibles and a lot of laughs in this book.

The Crazy World of Love. £3.99. By Roland Fiddy. This funny yet tender collection covers every aspect of love from its first joys to its dying embers. An ideal gift for lovers of all ages to share with each other.

The Crazy World of Marriage. £3.99. By Bill Stott. The battle of the sexes in close-up from the altar to the grave, in public and in private, in and out of bed. See your friends, your enemies (and possibly yourselves?) as never before!

The Crazy World of Music. £3.99. By Bill Stott. This upbeat collection will delight music-lovers of all ages. From Beethoven to Wagner and from star conductor to the humblest orchestra member, no-one escapes Bill Stott's penetrating pen.

The Crazy World of the Office. £3.99. By Bill Stott. Laugh your way through the office jungle with Bill Stott as he observes the idiosyncrasies of bosses, the deviousness of underlings and the goings-on at the Christmas party. ... A must for anyone who has ever worked in an office!

The Crazy World of Photography. £3.99. By Bill Stott. Everyone who owns a camera, be it a Box Brownie or the latest Pentax, will find something to laugh at in this superb collection. The absurdities of the camera freak will delight your whole family.

The Crazy World of Rugby. £3.99. By Bill Stott. From schoolboy to top international player, no-one who plays or watches rugby will escape Bill Stott's merciless exposé of their habits and absurdities. Over 80 hilarious cartoons – a must for all addicts.

The Crazy World of Sailing. £3.99. By Peter Rigby. The perfect present for anyone who has ever messed about in boats, gone pea-green in a storm or been stuck in the doldrums.

The Crazy World of Sex. £3.99. By David Pye. A light-hearted look at the absurdities and weaker moments of human passion – the turn-ons and the turn-offs. Very funny and in (reasonably) good taste.

The Crazy World of Skiing. £3.99. By Craig Peterson and Jerry Emerson. Covering almost every possible (and impossible) experience on the slopes, this is an ideal present for anyone who has ever strapped on skis – and instantly fallen over.

The Crazy World of Tennis. £3.99. By Peter Rigby. Would-be Pat Cashes and Chris Everts watch out.... This brilliant collection will pin-point their pretensions and poses. Whether you play yourself or only watch on TV, this will amuse and entertain you!

United Kingdom
These books make super presents. Order them from your local bookseller or from Exley Publications Ltd, Dept BP, 16 Chalk Hill, Watford, Herts WD1 4BN. (Please send £1.00 to cover post and packing.)
United States
All these titles are distributed in the United States by Slawson Communications Inc., 165 Vallecitos de Oro, San Marcos, CA 92069 and are priced at $8.95 each.